THRIVE HAIR THRIVE!

A workbook to help you thrive in your hair care journey and develop a kick-butt hair care routine!

Andrea D Boyd

Designed by: Andrea D Boyd

Let's Connect:

YOUTUBE.COM/SIMPLYDREA
INSTAGRAM: @ITSANDREADENISE

Copyright © 2019 Andrea D. Boyd
Published and designed by Andrea D Boyd

All rights reserved. All Rights reserved. No part of this publication may be reproduced, stored in a transmittal system, copied, or transmitted in any form or by any means, photocopying, elec-tronic, mechanical, or otherwise without the prior written consent of the author. Anyone found infringing upon or violating this copyright notice shall be pursued and prosecuted to the fullest extent of state and federal law and in accordance with the United States Constitution

ISBN (Paperback) : 978-0-9600273-3-0
ISBN: (ebook) : 978-0-9600273-4-7

IF THIS WORKBOOK IS EVER LOST, PLEASE CONTACT:

Name:

_____

Number:

_____

Social Media Handles:

_____

Email:

_____

Hey Sis!

Welcome to your new hair care best friend! A lot of times, we think we aren't making progress but we simply are not tracking our progress to have anything to compare it to. This workbook is designed to help you stay on track in your hair care journey. I highly recommend that you document EVERYTHING! This will help you to know what is working within your hair care routine and what is not. The sooner we figure that out, the better! If you use a product and notice benefits write it down and see how your hair continues to respond to it as you continue to use it. On the contrary, if you use a product or technique and notice a negative effect, add it to this workbook so that you remember what your hair did not like as well.

Remember, this workbook will not work unless you do so let's do this sis! It's time for us to step up our hair care game and create a kick-butt routine to help our hair thrive and to do that, we'll need to be consistent! It's time, and the time is now so let's get started!

Happy Hair Growing!

Andrea Denise

Youtube.com/simplydrea

HOW THE  WORKBOOK WORKS

You will notice several sections within this workbook so let's go through them so that you can utilize this workbook to its fullest potential.

CALENDARS:

Write out your routine for the week and month. This will take out the guesswork when it's time for wash day or a hot oil treatment. Again, remember to be as detailed as possible!

PRODUCT PAGES:

Jot down which products you're using and how your hair feels afterwards. This will help you big time, in the long run!

QUESTION PAGES:

Write down any questions you have or come across and send them to me on Instagram (@itsAndreaDenise) and in our Facebook Group (fb.me/AndreaDeniseSquad) with the initial title being "Thriving Hair"! No question is too small or big, so ask away and let's chat!

RECOMMENDATIONS:

These are simply my recommendations and what has and is working well for my hair. Your hair may be different from mine, so customize your routine to your hair and what will work best!

NOTES:

Write down EVERYTHING! This way, you know what's working and what isn't and you don't have to think back to what you did or didn't do to achieve results.

QUOTES:

I hope you can hear my voice through these quotes and motivational sayings! I'm truly cheering you on and can hardly wait to see your progress! Be sure to send me your before and after photos so I can celebrate with you. You got this sis!

TESTIMONIALS AND QUOTES

"I'm so glad I found and subscribed to your channel. My hair was in such bad shape. I suffered breakage and it felt rough but since my last relaxer and seeing your videos my hair is improving so much. Thank you!"

—Maria C.

"It's sooooooo good to have a relaxed hair content creator. I was starting to think I'd have to go natural just to take care of my hair. Thank God for you!"

- Ifeoluwa S.

HEALTHY HAIR OVER LENGTH BECAUSE HEALTHY HAIR GROWS!

- Andrea Denise

"My hair has grown because of the hair tips you give .. So thank u so much!"

- Latricia T.

"YOU have helped me to really grow my hair. I use ALL the products you mention and I really thank you!"

— Catina B.

I'M SO THANKFUL FOR THE WAY GOD HAS USED ME TO HELP THOUSANDS OF WOMEN! IT TRULY IS A BLESSING!

— Andrea Denise

I TRULY HOPE THAT MY CONTENT HELPS WOMEN FEEL MORE CONFIDENT WITH THEIR HAIR AND LIFE OVERALL. EVERY WOMAN IS BEAUTIFUL IN HER OWN WAY AND I HOPE SHE KNOWS THAT AND NEVER FORGETS IT!

— Andrea Denise

"Your videos have helped me in my relaxed hair journey, thank you!!! It's so nice to find videos with useful content on how to have healthy hair."

— Alexia B.

"Love your videos! I started my hair journey I'm January and your videos have helped me learn how to moisturize and seal."

— Asante B.

YOUTUBE.COM/ SIMPLYDREA

Recommended Products and Helpful tools

MOISTURIZERS
Mielle Moisturizing Avocado Hair Milk

Shea Moisture Curl Enhancing Smoothie

ORS Moisturizing Hair Lotion

SHAMPOOS
ORS Olive Oil Creamy Aloe Shampoo

Pomegranate & Honey by Mielle

CARRIER OILS
Castor Oil

Coconut Oil

Olive Oil

ESSENTIAL OILS
Peppermint Oil

Lavender Oil

PROTEIN DEEP CONDITIONERS
ORS Hair mayonnaise

Shea Moisture JBCO Oil Strengthen & Restore Conditioner

MOISTURIZING DEEP CONDITIONERS
Shea Moisture Manuka Honey Masque

ORS Replenishing Conditioner (protein and moisture)

CONDITIONERS FOR CO-WASHING
Aussie Moist Conditioner

Herbal Essences Hello Hydration

PROTEIN LEAVE-IN CONDITIONERS
Cantu Shea Butter Leave-In Conditioning Repair Cream

MOISTURIZING LEAVE-IN CONDITIONERS
Mielle Pomegranate and Honey Leave-In Conditioner

ANDREA DENISE'S TIPS AND TRICKS
- I only straighten my hair 3-4 times per year
- I moisturize and seal my hair every day or every other day
- I apply Castor Oil to my scalp for thick hair and hair growth
- Protective styles are my best friend! Braidouts, Twistouts, Bantu Knots and Wigs!
- I drink a lot of water and eat foods that promote healthy hair growth - Check out my Inside Out Challenge where I show you how to grow your from the inside out! Email me for more details! Andrea@Simplydrea.com

LET'S GET STARTED!

START BY RESEARCHING AND TRYING NEW PRODUCTS THAT YOU WOULD LIKE TO USE FOR YOUR HAIR!

On the next page, write down current products that are working as well as new products you'd like to possibly incorporate into your routine!

WRITE DOWN YOUR ROUTINE FOR THIS MONTH AS WELL AS HOW OFTEN YOU'LL DO EACH STEP

Moisturizer

_____
_____
_____
_____
_____

Shampoo

Clarifying Shampoo:
_____

Moisturizing Shampoo:
_____
_____

Deep Conditioner

Moisture Based Deep Conditioner
_____
_____

Protein Based Deep Conditioner
_____
_____

Leave-in Conditioner

_____
_____
_____
_____
_____
_____
_____

Deep Treatments
Protein Treaments, Hair Masks, etc.

_____
_____
_____
_____
_____
_____
_____

Oils

_____
_____
_____
_____
_____
_____
_____

Extras
(Olaplex) ▶

Tools
(Comb, Plastic shower caps) ▶

▶

Notes:

Questions I have:

Currently, I am experiencing these problems with my hair:

Date: _____ / _____ / _____

Healthy Hair

New Products I'm trying

Product:	My Thoughts:

Date: _____/_____/_____

Hair Care Routine Day by Day

| Sunday | Monday | Tuesday | Wednesday |

Write down your hair care plan for the week with as much detail as possible.

Date: _____ / _____ / _____

Thursday	Friday	Saturday	Notes

Month

Notes:

Notes:

Date: _____ / _____ / _____

Let's Talk Hair Care | Daily Hair Care

What I've done for my hair today:

Products I've used

How my hair feels:

Date: _____/_____/_____

Let's Talk Hair Care | Daily Hair Care

What I've done for my hair today:

Products I've used

How my hair feels:

Date: _____/_____/_____

Let's Talk Hair Care | Daily Hair Care

What I've done for my hair today:

Products I've used

How my hair feels:

Date: _____ / _____ / _____

Let's Talk Hair Care | Daily Hair Care

What I've done for my hair today:

Products I've used

How my hair feels:

Date: _____/_____/_____

Let's Talk Hair Care | Daily Hair Care

What I've done for my hair today:

Products I've used

How my hair feels:

Date: _____/_____/_____

Let's Talk Hair Care | Daily Hair Care

What I've done for my hair today:

Products I've used

How my hair feels:

Date: _____ / _____ / _____

Let's Talk Hair Care | Daily Hair Care

What I've done for my hair today:

Products I've used

How my hair feels:

Date: _____/_____/_____

Let's Talk Hair Care | Daily Hair Care

What I've done for my hair today:

Products I've used

How my hair feels:

Date: _____ / _____ / _____

Let's Talk Hair Care | Daily Hair Care

What I've done for my hair today:

Products I've used

How my hair feels:

Date: _____/_____/_____

Let's Talk Hair Care | Daily Hair Care

What I've done for my hair today:

Products I've used

How my hair feels:

Date: _____/_____/_____

Let's Talk Hair Care | Daily Hair Care

What I've done for my hair today:

Products I've used

How my hair feels:

Date: _____/_____/_____

Let's Talk Hair Care | Daily Hair Care

What I've done for my hair today:

Products I've used

How my hair feels:

Date: _____ / _____ / _____

Let's Talk Hair Care | Daily Hair Care

What I've done for my hair today:

Products I've used

How my hair feels:

Date: _____ / _____ / _____

Let's Talk Hair Care | Daily Hair Care

What I've done for my hair today:

Products I've used

How my hair feels:

Date: _____/_____/_____

Let's Talk Hair Care | Daily Hair Care

What I've done for my hair today:

Products I've used

How my hair feels:

Date: _____/_____/_____

Let's Talk Hair Care | Daily Hair Care

What I've done for my hair today:

Products I've used

How my hair feels:

Date: _____ / _____ / _____

Let's Talk Hair Care | Daily Hair Care

What I've done for my hair today:

Products I've used

How my hair feels:

Date: _____/_____/_____

Let's Talk Hair Care | Daily Hair Care

What I've done for my hair today:

Products I've used

How my hair feels:

Date: _____/_____/_____

Let's Talk Hair Care | Daily Hair Care

What I've done for my hair today:

Products I've used

How my hair feels:

Date: _____/_____/_____

Let's Talk Hair Care | Daily Hair Care

What I've done for my hair today:

Products I've used

How my hair feels:

Date: _____/_____/_____

Let's Talk Hair Care | Daily Hair Care

What I've done for my hair today:

Products I've used

How my hair feels:

Date: _____ / _____ / _____

Let's Talk Hair Care | Daily Hair Care

What I've done for my hair today:

Products I've used

How my hair feels:

Date: _____ / _____ / _____

Let's Talk Hair Care | Daily Hair Care

What I've done for my hair today:

Products I've used

How my hair feels:

Date: _____/_____/_____

Let's Talk Hair Care | Daily Hair Care

What I've done for my hair today:

Products I've used

How my hair feels:

Date: _____ / _____ / _____

Let's Talk Hair Care | Daily Hair Care

What I've done for my hair today:

Products I've used

How my hair feels:

SIS, YOUR HAIR IS THRIVING!

Andrea Denise

Monthly RECAP

Date: _____/_____/_____

CHECKING IN

Compared to last month, my hair...

Products I loved this past month...

One new thing I learned about my hair is...

YOUR HAIR IS LOOKING GOOD, SIS!

Andrea Denise

WRITE DOWN YOUR ROUTINE FOR THIS MONTH AS WELL AS HOW OFTEN YOU'LL DO EACH STEP

Moisturizer ▶

_____
_____
_____
_____
_____

Shampoo ▶

Clarifying Shampoo:
_____
_____

Moisturizing Shampoo:
_____
_____
_____

Deep Conditioner ▶

Moisture Based Deep Conditioner
_____
_____
_____

Protein Based Deep Conditioner
_____
_____
_____

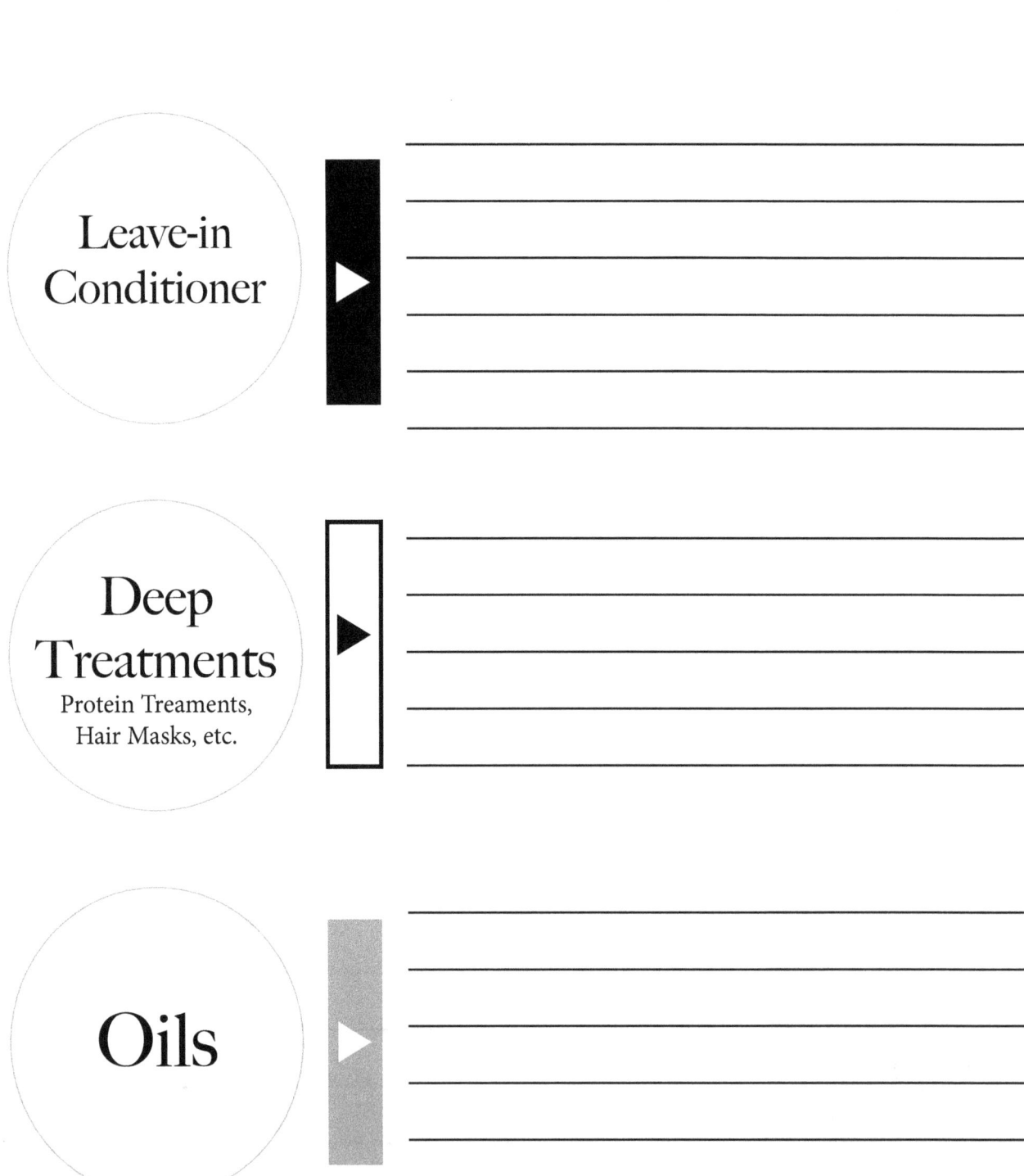

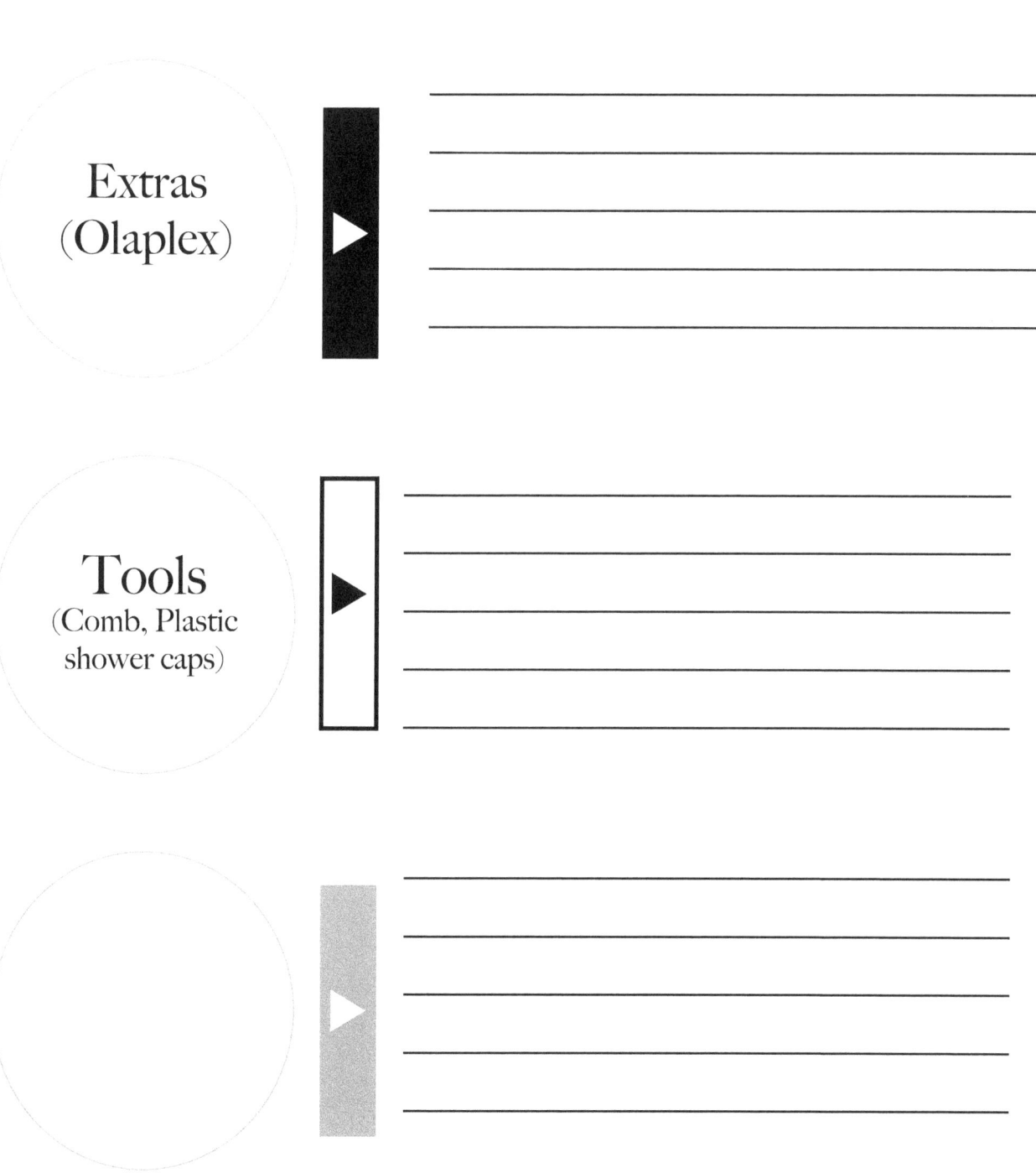

Notes:

Questions I have:

Date: _____ / _____ / _____

Currently, I am experiencing these problems with my hair:

Healthy Hair

New Products I'm trying

Product:	My Thoughts:

Date: _____/_____/_____

Hair Care Routine Day by Day

| Sunday | Monday | Tuesday | Wednesday |

Write down your hair care plan for the week with as much detail as possible.

Date: _____ / _____ / _____

Thursday	Friday	Saturday	Notes

Month

Notes:
_____
_____
_____
_____

Date: _____ / _____ / _____

Let's Talk Hair Care | Daily Hair Care

What I've done for my hair today:

Products I've used

How my hair feels:

Date: _____/_____/_____

Let's Talk Hair Care | Daily Hair Care

What I've done for my hair today:

Products I've used

How my hair feels:

Date: _____/_____/_____

Let's Talk Hair Care | Daily Hair Care

What I've done for my hair today:

Products I've used

How my hair feels:

Date: _____/_____/_____

Let's Talk Hair Care | Daily Hair Care

What I've done for my hair today:

Products I've used

How my hair feels:

Date: _____/_____/_____

Let's Talk Hair Care | Daily Hair Care

What I've done for my hair today:

Products I've used

How my hair feels:

Date: _____ / _____ / _____

Let's Talk Hair Care | Daily Hair Care

What I've done for my hair today:

Products I've used

How my hair feels:

Date: _____/_____/_____

Let's Talk Hair Care | Daily Hair Care

What I've done for my hair today:

Products I've used

How my hair feels:

Date: _____/_____/_____

Let's Talk Hair Care | Daily Hair Care

What I've done for my hair today:

Products I've used

How my hair feels:

Date: _____/_____/_____

Let's Talk Hair Care | Daily Hair Care

What I've done for my hair today:

Products I've used

How my hair feels:

Date: _____/_____/_____

Let's Talk Hair Care | Daily Hair Care

What I've done for my hair today:

Products I've used

How my hair feels:

Date: _____/_____/_____

Let's Talk Hair Care | Daily Hair Care

What I've done for my hair today:

Products I've used

How my hair feels:

Date: _____/_____/_____

Let's Talk Hair Care | Daily Hair Care

What I've done for my hair today:

Products I've used

How my hair feels:

Date: _____ / _____ / _____

Let's Talk Hair Care | Daily Hair Care

What I've done for my hair today:

Products I've used

How my hair feels:

Date: _____ / _____ / _____

Let's Talk Hair Care | Daily Hair Care

What I've done for my hair today:

Products I've used

How my hair feels:

Date: _____/_____/_____

Let's Talk Hair Care | Daily Hair Care

What I've done for my hair today:

Products I've used

How my hair feels:

Date: _____ / _____ / _____

Let's Talk Hair Care | Daily Hair Care

What I've done for my hair today:

Products I've used

How my hair feels:

Date: _____/_____/_____

Let's Talk Hair Care | Daily Hair Care

What I've done for my hair today:

Products I've used

How my hair feels:

Date: _____/_____/_____

Let's Talk Hair Care | Daily Hair Care

What I've done for my hair today:

Products I've used

How my hair feels:

Date: _____/_____/_____

Let's Talk Hair Care | Daily Hair Care

What I've done for my hair today:

Products I've used

How my hair feels:

Date: _____/_____/_____

Let's Talk Hair Care | Daily Hair Care

What I've done for my hair today:

Products I've used

How my hair feels:

Date: _____ / _____ / _____

Let's Talk Hair Care | Daily Hair Care

What I've done for my hair today:

Products I've used

How my hair feels:

Date: _____ / _____ / _____

Let's Talk Hair Care | Daily Hair Care

What I've done for my hair today:

Products I've used

How my hair feels:

Date: _____ / _____ / _____

Let's Talk Hair Care | Daily Hair Care

What I've done for my hair today:

Products I've used

How my hair feels:

Date: _____ / _____ / _____

Let's Talk Hair Care | Daily Hair Care

What I've done for my hair today:

Products I've used

How my hair feels:

Date: _____/_____/_____

Let's Talk Hair Care | Daily Hair Care

What I've done for my hair today:

Products I've used

How my hair feels:

Date: _____ / _____ / _____

Let's Talk Hair Care | Daily Hair Care

What I've done for my hair today:

Products I've used

How my hair feels:

Date: _____ / _____ / _____

Let's Talk Hair Care | Daily Hair Care

What I've done for my hair today:

Products I've used

How my hair feels:

Date: _____ / _____ / _____

Let's Talk Hair Care | Daily Hair Care

What I've done for my hair today:

Products I've used

How my hair feels:

Date: _____ / _____ / _____

Let's Talk Hair Care | Daily Hair Care

What I've done for my hair today:

Products I've used

How my hair feels:

Date: _____/_____/_____

Let's Talk Hair Care | Daily Hair Care

What I've done for my hair today:

Products I've used

How my hair feels:

Date: _____/_____/_____

Let's Talk Hair Care | Daily Hair Care

What I've done for my hair today:

Products I've used

How my hair feels:

Monthly RECAP

Date: _____/_____/_____

Compared to last month, my hair...

CHECKING IN

Products I loved this past month...

One new thing I learned about my hair is...

YES YOU CAN!

Andrea Denise

WRITE DOWN YOUR ROUTINE FOR THIS MONTH AS WELL AS HOW OFTEN YOU'LL DO EACH STEP

Moisturizer ▶

_____
_____
_____
_____
_____

Shampoo ▶

Clarifying Shampoo:
_____
_____

Moisturizing Shampoo:
_____
_____
_____

Deep Conditioner ▶

Moisture Based Deep Conditioner
_____
_____
_____

Protein Based Deep Conditioner
_____
_____
_____

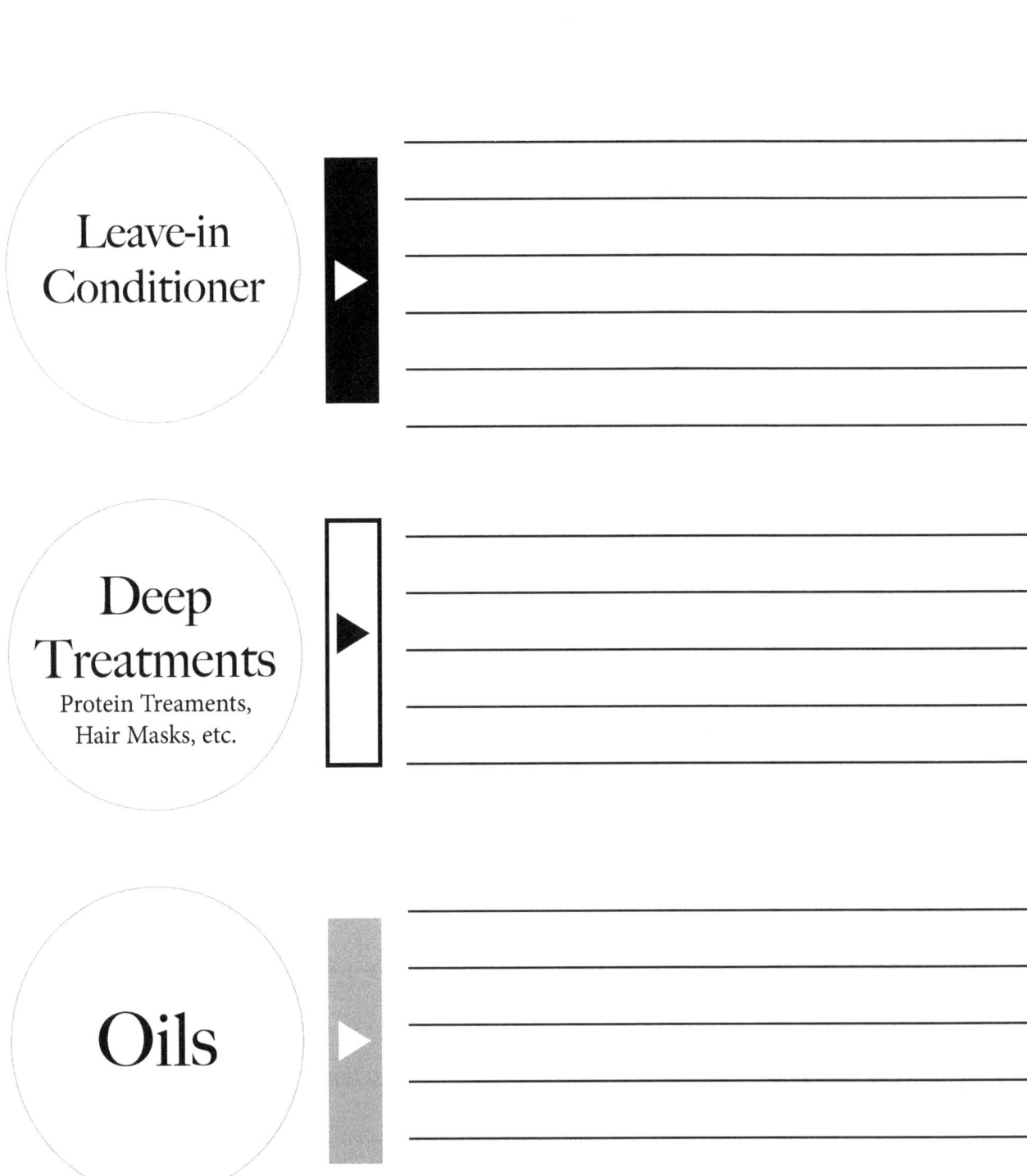

Extras
(Olaplex)

_____
_____
_____
_____
_____

Tools
(Comb, Plastic shower caps)

_____
_____
_____
_____
_____

_____
_____
_____
_____
_____

Notes:

Questions I have:

Date: _____ / _____ / _____

Currently, I am experiencing these problems with my hair:

Healthy Hair

New Products I'm trying

Product:	My Thoughts:

Date: _____/_____/_____

Hair Care Routine Day by Day

| Sunday | Monday | Tuesday | Wednesday |

Write down your hair care plan for the week with as much detail as possible.

Date: _____/_____/_____

Thursday	Friday	Saturday	Notes

Month

Notes:
___
___
___
___

Date: _____/_____/_____

Let's Talk Hair Care | Daily Hair Care

What I've done for my hair today:

Products I've used

How my hair feels:

Date: _____ / _____ / _____

Let's Talk Hair Care | Daily Hair Care

What I've done for my hair today:

Products I've used

How my hair feels:

Date: _____/_____/_____

Let's Talk Hair Care | Daily Hair Care

What I've done for my hair today:

Products I've used

How my hair feels:

Date: _____/_____/_____

Let's Talk Hair Care | Daily Hair Care

What I've done for my hair today:

Products I've used

How my hair feels:

Date: _____/_____/_____

Let's Talk Hair Care | Daily Hair Care

What I've done for my hair today:

Products I've used

How my hair feels:

Date: _____ / _____ / _____

Let's Talk Hair Care | Daily Hair Care

What I've done for my hair today:

Products I've used

How my hair feels:

Date: _____/_____/_____

Let's Talk Hair Care | Daily Hair Care

What I've done for my hair today:

Products I've used

How my hair feels:

Date: _____/_____/_____

Let's Talk Hair Care | Daily Hair Care

What I've done for my hair today:

Products I've used

How my hair feels:

Date: _____ / _____ / _____

Let's Talk Hair Care | Daily Hair Care

What I've done for my hair today:

Products I've used

How my hair feels:

Date: _____/_____/_____

Let's Talk Hair Care | Daily Hair Care

What I've done for my hair today:

Products I've used

How my hair feels:

Date: _____ / _____ / _____

Let's Talk Hair Care | Daily Hair Care

What I've done for my hair today:

Products I've used

How my hair feels:

Date: _____ / _____ / _____

Let's Talk Hair Care | Daily Hair Care

What I've done for my hair today:

Products I've used

How my hair feels:

Date: _____ / _____ / _____

Let's Talk Hair Care | Daily Hair Care

What I've done for my hair today:

Products I've used

How my hair feels:

Date: _____/_____/_____

Let's Talk Hair Care | Daily Hair Care

What I've done for my hair today:

Products I've used

How my hair feels:

Date: _____ / _____ / _____

Let's Talk Hair Care | Daily Hair Care

What I've done for my hair today:

Products I've used

How my hair feels:

Date: _____/_____/_____

Let's Talk Hair Care | Daily Hair Care

What I've done for my hair today:

Products I've used

How my hair feels:

Date: _____/_____/_____

Let's Talk Hair Care | Daily Hair Care

What I've done for my hair today:

Products I've used

How my hair feels:

Date: _____ / _____ / _____

Let's Talk Hair Care | Daily Hair Care

What I've done for my hair today:

Products I've used

How my hair feels:

Date: _____/_____/_____

Let's Talk Hair Care | Daily Hair Care

What I've done for my hair today:

Products I've used

How my hair feels:

Date: _____/_____/_____

Let's Talk Hair Care | Daily Hair Care

What I've done for my hair today:

Products I've used

How my hair feels:

Date: _____/_____/_____

Let's Talk Hair Care | Daily Hair Care

What I've done for my hair today:

Products I've used

How my hair feels:

Date: _____/_____/_____

Let's Talk Hair Care | Daily Hair Care

What I've done for my hair today:

Products I've used

How my hair feels:

Date: _____/_____/_____

Let's Talk Hair Care | Daily Hair Care

What I've done for my hair today:

Products I've used

How my hair feels:

Date: _____/_____/_____

Let's Talk Hair Care | Daily Hair Care

What I've done for my hair today:

Products I've used

How my hair feels:

Date: _____/_____/_____

Let's Talk Hair Care | Daily Hair Care

What I've done for my hair today:

Products I've used

How my hair feels:

Date: _____/_____/_____

Let's Talk Hair Care | Daily Hair Care

What I've done for my hair today:

Products I've used

How my hair feels:

Date: _____/_____/_____

Let's Talk Hair Care | Daily Hair Care

What I've done for my hair today:

Products I've used

How my hair feels:

Date: _____ / _____ / _____

Let's Talk Hair Care | Daily Hair Care

What I've done for my hair today:

Products I've used

How my hair feels:

Date: _____/_____/_____

Let's Talk Hair Care | Daily Hair Care

What I've done for my hair today:

Products I've used

How my hair feels:

Date: _____/_____/_____

Let's Talk Hair Care | Daily Hair Care

What I've done for my hair today:

Products I've used

How my hair feels:

Date: _____ / _____ / _____

Let's Talk Hair Care | Daily Hair Care

What I've done for my hair today:

Products I've used

How my hair feels:

Date: _____/_____/_____

Let's Talk Hair Care | Daily Hair Care

What I've done for my hair today:

Products I've used

How my hair feels:

Monthly RECAP

Date: _____/_____/_____

CHECKING IN

Compared to last month, my hair...

Products I loved this past month...

One new thing I learned about my hair is...

DON'T FORGET TO TAKE PROGRESS PICTURES!

WRITE DOWN YOUR ROUTINE FOR THIS MONTH AS WELL AS HOW OFTEN YOU'LL DO EACH STEP

Moisturizer ▶
_____
_____
_____
_____
_____

Shampoo ▶
Clarifying Shampoo: _____
_____
Moisturizing Shampoo: _____
_____
_____

Deep Conditioner ▶
Moisture Based Deep Conditioner _____
_____
_____
Protein Based Deep Conditioner _____
_____
_____

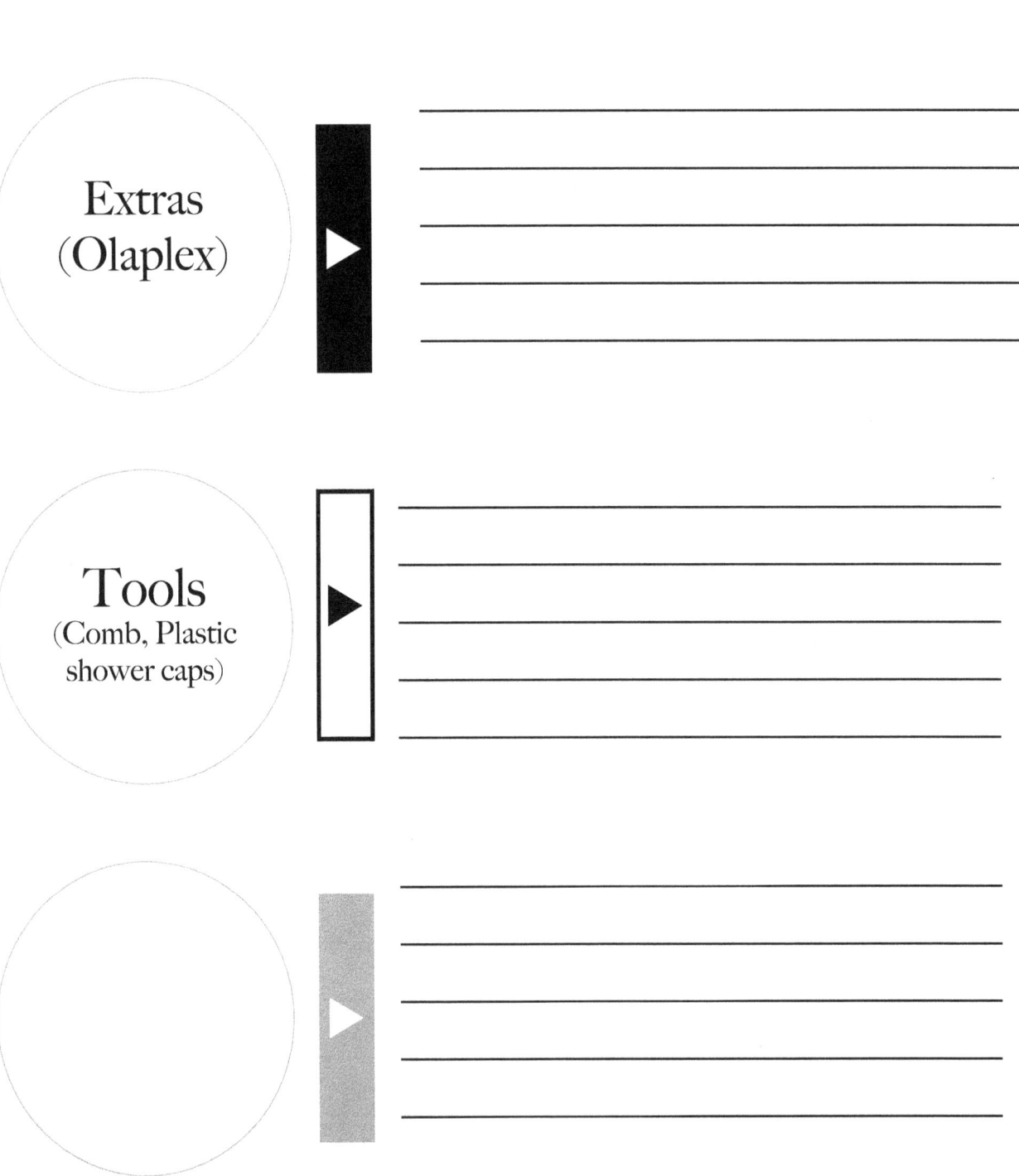

Questions I have:

Date: _____/_____/_____

Currently, I am experiencing these problems with my hair:

Healthy Hair

New Products I'm trying

Product:	My Thoughts:

Notes:

Date: _____/_____/_____

Hair Care Routine Day by Day

Sunday	Monday	Tuesday	Wednesday

Write down your hair care plan for the week with as much detail as possible.

Date: _____/_____/_____

Thursday	Friday	Saturday	Notes

Month

Notes:
_____
_____
_____
_____

Date: _____ / _____ / _____

Let's Talk Hair Care | Daily Hair Care

What I've done for my hair today:

Products I've used

How my hair feels:

Date: _____/_____/_____

Let's Talk Hair Care | Daily Hair Care

What I've done for my hair today:

Products I've used

How my hair feels:

Date: _____ / _____ / _____

Let's Talk Hair Care | Daily Hair Care

What I've done for my hair today:

Products I've used

How my hair feels:

Date: _____/_____/_____

Let's Talk Hair Care | Daily Hair Care

What I've done for my hair today:

Products I've used

How my hair feels:

Date: _____ / _____ / _____

Let's Talk Hair Care | Daily Hair Care

What I've done for my hair today:

Products I've used

How my hair feels:

Date: _____ / _____ / _____

Let's Talk Hair Care | Daily Hair Care

What I've done for my hair today:

Products I've used

How my hair feels:

Date: _____/_____/_____

Let's Talk Hair Care | Daily Hair Care

What I've done for my hair today:

Products I've used

How my hair feels:

Date: _____ / _____ / _____

Let's Talk Hair Care | Daily Hair Care

What I've done for my hair today:

Products I've used

How my hair feels:

Date: _____/_____/_____

Let's Talk Hair Care | Daily Hair Care

What I've done for my hair today:

Products I've used

How my hair feels:

Date: _____/_____/_____

Let's Talk Hair Care | Daily Hair Care

What I've done for my hair today:

Products I've used

How my hair feels:

Date: _____ / _____ / _____

Let's Talk Hair Care | Daily Hair Care

What I've done for my hair today:

Products I've used

How my hair feels:

Date: _____ / _____ / _____

Let's Talk Hair Care | Daily Hair Care

What I've done for my hair today:

Products I've used

How my hair feels:

Date: _____ / _____ / _____

Let's Talk Hair Care | Daily Hair Care

What I've done for my hair today:

Products I've used

How my hair feels:

Date: _____/_____/_____

Let's Talk Hair Care | Daily Hair Care

What I've done for my hair today:

Products I've used

How my hair feels:

Date: _____/_____/_____

Let's Talk Hair Care | Daily Hair Care

What I've done for my hair today:

Products I've used

How my hair feels:

Date: _____ / _____ / _____

Let's Talk Hair Care | Daily Hair Care

What I've done for my hair today:

Products I've used

How my hair feels:

Date: _____/_____/_____

Let's Talk Hair Care | Daily Hair Care

What I've done for my hair today:

Products I've used

How my hair feels:

Date: _____/_____/_____

Let's Talk Hair Care | Daily Hair Care

What I've done for my hair today:

Products I've used

How my hair feels:

Date: _____/_____/_____

Let's Talk Hair Care | Daily Hair Care

What I've done for my hair today:

Products I've used

How my hair feels:

Date: _____/_____/_____

Let's Talk Hair Care | Daily Hair Care

What I've done for my hair today:

Products I've used

How my hair feels:

Date: _____/_____/_____

Let's Talk Hair Care | Daily Hair Care

What I've done for my hair today:

Products I've used

How my hair feels:

Date: _____/_____/_____

Let's Talk Hair Care | Daily Hair Care

What I've done for my hair today:

Products I've used

How my hair feels:

Date: _____/_____/_____

Let's Talk Hair Care | Daily Hair Care

What I've done for my hair today:

Products I've used

How my hair feels:

Date: _____/_____/_____

Let's Talk Hair Care | Daily Hair Care

What I've done for my hair today:

Products I've used

How my hair feels:

Date: _____ / _____ / _____

Let's Talk Hair Care | Daily Hair Care

What I've done for my hair today:

Products I've used

How my hair feels:

Date: _____ / _____ / _____

Let's Talk Hair Care | Daily Hair Care

What I've done for my hair today:

Products I've used

How my hair feels:

Date: _____ / _____ / _____

Let's Talk Hair Care | Daily Hair Care

What I've done for my hair today:

Products I've used

How my hair feels:

Date: _____ / _____ / _____

Let's Talk Hair Care | Daily Hair Care

What I've done for my hair today:

Products I've used

How my hair feels:

Date: _____ / _____ / _____

Let's Talk Hair Care | Daily Hair Care

What I've done for my hair today:

Products I've used

How my hair feels:

Date: _____/_____/_____

Let's Talk Hair Care | Daily Hair Care

What I've done for my hair today:

Products I've used

How my hair feels:

Date: _____/_____/_____

Let's Talk Hair Care | Daily Hair Care

What I've done for my hair today:

Products I've used

How my hair feels:

Monthly RECAP

Date: _____ / _____ / _____

CHECKING IN

Compared to last month, my hair...

Products I loved this past month...

One new thing I learned about my hair is...

I KNOW YOU CAN DO THIS

Andrea Denise

WRITE DOWN YOUR ROUTINE FOR THIS MONTH AS WELL AS HOW OFTEN YOU'LL DO EACH STEP

Moisturizer ▶
_____
_____
_____
_____
_____

Shampoo ▶
Clarifying Shampoo: _____
_____
Moisturizing Shampoo: _____
_____
_____

Deep Conditioner ▶
Moisture Based Deep Conditioner
_____
_____
Protein Based Deep Conditioner
_____
_____

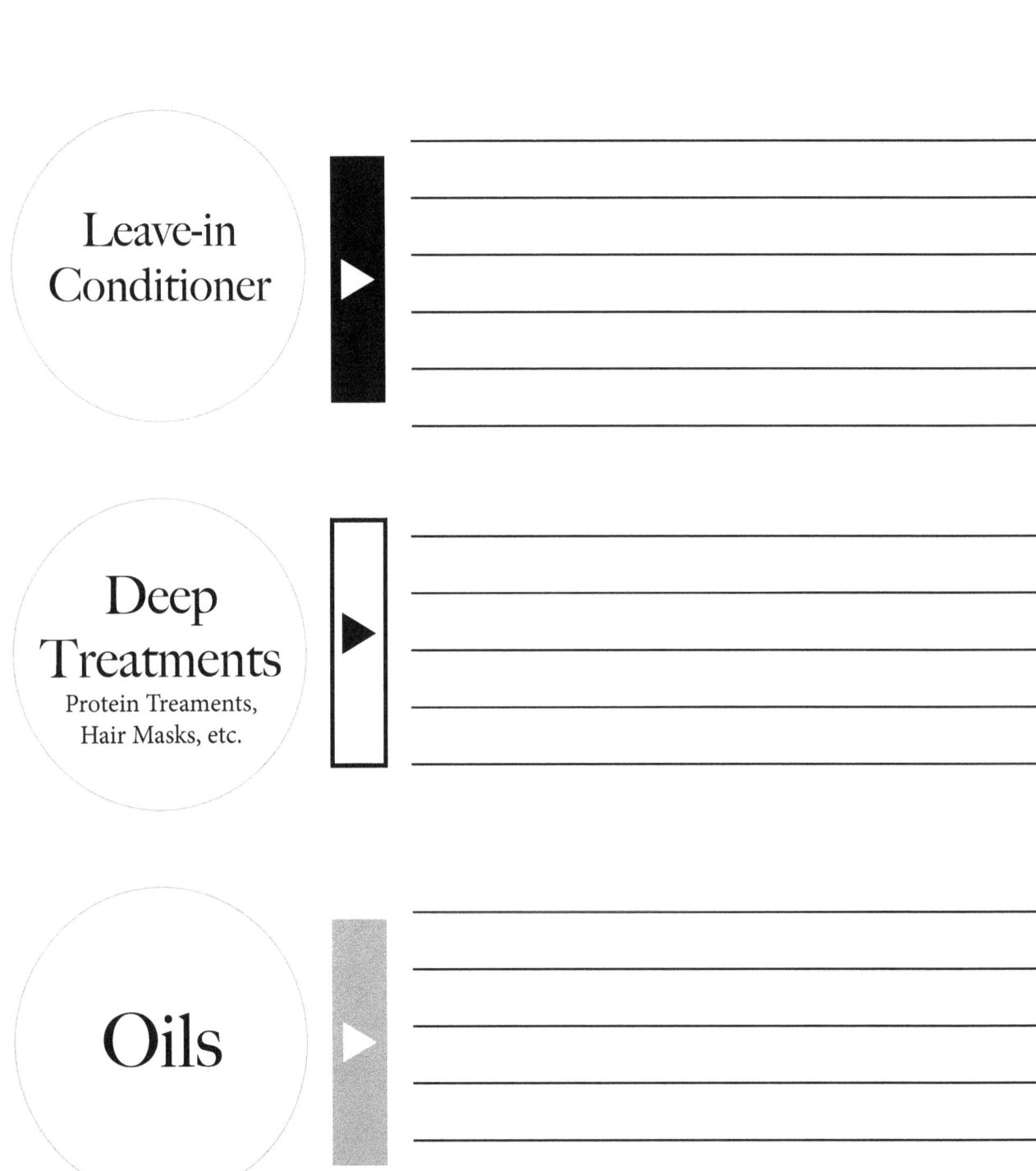

Extras
(Olaplex)

Tools
(Comb, Plastic shower caps)

Questions I have:

Date: _____/_____/_____

Currently, I am experiencing these problems with my hair:

Healthy Hair

New Products I'm trying

Product:	My Thoughts:

Date: _____/_____/_____

Hair Care Routine Day by Day

| Sunday | Monday | Tuesday | Wednesday |

Write down your hair care plan for the week with as much detail as possible.

Date: _____/_____/_____

Thursday	Friday	Saturday	Notes

Month

Notes:

_____
_____
_____
_____

Date: _____/_____/_____

Let's Talk Hair Care | Daily Hair Care

What I've done for my hair today:

Products I've used

How my hair feels:

Date: _____/_____/_____

Let's Talk Hair Care | Daily Hair Care

What I've done for my hair today:

Products I've used

How my hair feels:

Date: _____/_____/_____

Let's Talk Hair Care | Daily Hair Care

What I've done for my hair today:

Products I've used

How my hair feels:

Date: _____/_____/_____

Let's Talk Hair Care | Daily Hair Care

What I've done for my hair today:

Products I've used

How my hair feels:

Date: _____ / _____ / _____

Let's Talk Hair Care | Daily Hair Care

What I've done for my hair today:

Products I've used

How my hair feels:

Date: _____ / _____ / _____

Let's Talk Hair Care | Daily Hair Care

What I've done for my hair today:

Products I've used

How my hair feels:

Date: _____/_____/_____

Let's Talk Hair Care | Daily Hair Care

What I've done for my hair today:

Products I've used

How my hair feels:

Date: _____/_____/_____

Let's Talk Hair Care | Daily Hair Care

What I've done for my hair today:

Products I've used

How my hair feels:

Date: _____/_____/_____

Let's Talk Hair Care | Daily Hair Care

What I've done for my hair today:

Products I've used

How my hair feels:

Date: _____/_____/_____

Let's Talk Hair Care | Daily Hair Care

What I've done for my hair today:

Products I've used

How my hair feels:

Date: _____/_____/_____

Let's Talk Hair Care | Daily Hair Care

What I've done for my hair today:

Products I've used

How my hair feels:

Date: _____ / _____ / _____

Let's Talk Hair Care | Daily Hair Care

What I've done for my hair today:

Products I've used

How my hair feels:

Date: _____ / _____ / _____

Let's Talk Hair Care | Daily Hair Care

What I've done for my hair today:

Products I've used

How my hair feels:

DON'T GIVE UP! YOU'VE GOT THIS

Date: _____ / _____ / _____

Let's Talk Hair Care | Daily Hair Care

What I've done for my hair today:

Products I've used

How my hair feels:

Date: _____ / _____ / _____

Let's Talk Hair Care | Daily Hair Care

What I've done for my hair today:

Products I've used

How my hair feels:

Date: _____ / _____ / _____

Let's Talk Hair Care | Daily Hair Care

What I've done for my hair today:

Products I've used

How my hair feels:

Date: _____/_____/_____

Let's Talk Hair Care | Daily Hair Care

What I've done for my hair today:

Products I've used

How my hair feels:

Date: _____ / _____ / _____

Let's Talk Hair Care | Daily Hair Care

What I've done for my hair today:

Products I've used

How my hair feels:

Date: _____ / _____ / _____

Let's Talk Hair Care | Daily Hair Care

What I've done for my hair today:

Products I've used

How my hair feels:

Date: _____/_____/_____

Let's Talk Hair Care | Daily Hair Care

What I've done for my hair today:

Products I've used

How my hair feels:

Date: _____/_____/_____

Let's Talk Hair Care | Daily Hair Care

What I've done for my hair today:

Products I've used

How my hair feels:

Date: _____/_____/_____

Let's Talk Hair Care | Daily Hair Care

What I've done for my hair today:

Products I've used

How my hair feels:

Date: _____ / _____ / _____

Let's Talk Hair Care | Daily Hair Care

What I've done for my hair today:

Products I've used

How my hair feels:

Date: _____/_____/_____

Let's Talk Hair Care | Daily Hair Care

What I've done for my hair today:

Products I've used

How my hair feels:

Date: _____/_____/_____

Let's Talk Hair Care | Daily Hair Care

What I've done for my hair today:

Products I've used

How my hair feels:

Date: _____ / _____ / _____

Let's Talk Hair Care | Daily Hair Care

What I've done for my hair today:

Products I've used

How my hair feels:

Date: _____/_____/_____

Let's Talk Hair Care | Daily Hair Care

What I've done for my hair today:

Products I've used

How my hair feels:

Date: _____/_____/_____

Let's Talk Hair Care | Daily Hair Care

What I've done for my hair today:

Products I've used

How my hair feels:

Date: _____/_____/_____

Let's Talk Hair Care | Daily Hair Care

What I've done for my hair today:

Products I've used

How my hair feels:

Date: _____/_____/_____

Let's Talk Hair Care | Daily Hair Care

What I've done for my hair today:

Products I've used

How my hair feels:

Date: _____/_____/_____

Let's Talk Hair Care | Daily Hair Care

What I've done for my hair today:

Products I've used

How my hair feels:

Date: _____/_____/_____

Let's Talk Hair Care | Daily Hair Care

What I've done for my hair today:

Products I've used

How my hair feels:

Monthly RECAP

Date: _____ / _____ / _____

Compared to last month, my hair...

CHECKING IN

Products I loved this past month...

One new thing I learned about my hair is...

I KNOW YOU CAN DO THIS

Andrea Denise

WRITE DOWN YOUR ROUTINE FOR THIS MONTH AS WELL AS HOW OFTEN YOU'LL DO EACH STEP

Moisturizer

_____
_____
_____
_____
_____

Shampoo

Clarifying Shampoo: _____
_____

Moisturizing Shampoo: _____
_____
_____

Deep Conditioner

Moisture Based Deep Conditioner
_____
_____
_____

Protein Based Deep Conditioner
_____
_____
_____

Leave-in Conditioner

_____
_____
_____
_____
_____
_____
_____

Deep Treatments
Protein Treaments, Hair Masks, etc.

_____
_____
_____
_____
_____
_____
_____

Oils

_____
_____
_____
_____
_____
_____
_____

Extras
(Olaplex)

_____
_____
_____
_____
_____
_____

Tools
(Comb, Plastic shower caps)

_____
_____
_____
_____
_____
_____

_____
_____
_____
_____
_____
_____

Notes:

Questions I have:

Date: _____ / _____ / _____

Currently, I am experiencing these problems with my hair:

Healthy Hair

New Products I'm trying

Product:	My Thoughts:

Date: _____/_____/_____

Hair Care Routine Day by Day

Sunday	Monday	Tuesday	Wednesday

Write down your hair care plan for the week with as much detail as possible.

Date: _____/_____/_____

Thursday	Friday	Saturday	Notes

Month

Notes:

Date: _____/_____/_____

Let's Talk Hair Care | Daily Hair Care

What I've done for my hair today:

Products I've used

How my hair feels:

Date: _____ / _____ / _____

Let's Talk Hair Care | Daily Hair Care

What I've done for my hair today:

Products I've used

How my hair feels:

Date: _____/_____/_____

Let's Talk Hair Care | Daily Hair Care

What I've done for my hair today:

Products I've used

How my hair feels:

Date: _____/_____/_____

Let's Talk Hair Care | Daily Hair Care

What I've done for my hair today:

Products I've used

How my hair feels:

Date: _____/_____/_____

Let's Talk Hair Care | Daily Hair Care

What I've done for my hair today:

Products I've used

How my hair feels:

Date: _____ / _____ / _____

Let's Talk Hair Care | Daily Hair Care

What I've done for my hair today:

Products I've used

How my hair feels:

Date: _____ / _____ / _____

Let's Talk Hair Care | Daily Hair Care

What I've done for my hair today:

Products I've used

How my hair feels:

Date: _____/_____/_____

Let's Talk Hair Care | Daily Hair Care

What I've done for my hair today:

Products I've used

How my hair feels:

Date: _____/_____/_____

Let's Talk Hair Care | Daily Hair Care

What I've done for my hair today:

Products I've used

How my hair feels:

Date: _____ / _____ / _____

Let's Talk Hair Care | Daily Hair Care

What I've done for my hair today:

Products I've used

How my hair feels:

Date: _____/_____/_____

Let's Talk Hair Care | Daily Hair Care

What I've done for my hair today:

Products I've used

How my hair feels:

Date: _____ / _____ / _____

Let's Talk Hair Care | Daily Hair Care

What I've done for my hair today:

Products I've used

How my hair feels:

Date: _____/_____/_____

Let's Talk Hair Care | Daily Hair Care

What I've done for my hair today:

Products I've used

How my hair feels:

Date: _____/_____/_____

Let's Talk Hair Care | Daily Hair Care

What I've done for my hair today:

Products I've used

How my hair feels:

Date: _____ / _____ / _____

Let's Talk Hair Care | Daily Hair Care

What I've done for my hair today:

Products I've used

How my hair feels:

Date: _____/_____/_____

Let's Talk Hair Care | Daily Hair Care

What I've done for my hair today:

Products I've used

How my hair feels:

Date: _____/_____/_____

Let's Talk Hair Care | Daily Hair Care

What I've done for my hair today:

Products I've used

How my hair feels:

Date: _____ / _____ / _____

Let's Talk Hair Care | Daily Hair Care

What I've done for my hair today:

Products I've used

How my hair feels:

Date: _____/_____/_____

Let's Talk Hair Care | Daily Hair Care

What I've done for my hair today:

Products I've used

How my hair feels:

Date: _____ / _____ / _____

Let's Talk Hair Care | Daily Hair Care

What I've done for my hair today:

Products I've used

How my hair feels:

Date: _____/_____/_____

Let's Talk Hair Care | Daily Hair Care

What I've done for my hair today:

Products I've used

How my hair feels:

Date: _____/_____/_____

Let's Talk Hair Care | Daily Hair Care

What I've done for my hair today:

Products I've used

How my hair feels:

Date: _____ / _____ / _____

Let's Talk Hair Care | Daily Hair Care

What I've done for my hair today:

Products I've used

How my hair feels:

Date: _____/_____/_____

Let's Talk Hair Care | Daily Hair Care

What I've done for my hair today:

Products I've used

How my hair feels:

Date: _____/_____/_____

Let's Talk Hair Care | Daily Hair Care

What I've done for my hair today:

Products I've used

How my hair feels:

Date: _____ / _____ / _____

Let's Talk Hair Care | Daily Hair Care

What I've done for my hair today:

Products I've used

How my hair feels:

Date: _____/_____/_____

Let's Talk Hair Care | Daily Hair Care

What I've done for my hair today:

Products I've used

How my hair feels:

Date: _____/_____/_____

Let's Talk Hair Care | Daily Hair Care

What I've done for my hair today:

Products I've used

How my hair feels:

Date: _____/_____/_____

Let's Talk Hair Care | Daily Hair Care

What I've done for my hair today:

Products I've used

How my hair feels:

Date: _____ / _____ / _____

Let's Talk Hair Care | Daily Hair Care

What I've done for my hair today:

Products I've used

How my hair feels:

Date: _____/_____/_____

Let's Talk Hair Care | Daily Hair Care

What I've done for my hair today:

Products I've used

How my hair feels:

Date: _____ / _____ / _____

Let's Talk Hair Care | Daily Hair Care

What I've done for my hair today:

Products I've used

How my hair feels:

Monthly RECAP

Date: _____/_____/_____

CHECKING IN

Compared to last month, my hair...

Products I loved this past month...

One new thing I learned about my hair is...

LOOK HOW FAR YOU'VE COME! I'M SO PROUD OF YOU!

Andrea Denise

www.ingramcontent.com/pod-product-compliance
Lightning Source LLC
Chambersburg PA
CBHW080604080426
42453CB00031B/2272